THE BRUCE TRAIL COUNTRY
Niagara to Tobermory

Photographs by Peter Fowler
Introduction by Martin Keen

Toronto
OXFORD UNIVERSITY PRESS
1980

Designed by FORTUNATO AGLIALORO

©Oxford University Press (Canadian Branch) 1980
ISBN 0-19-540345-2
1 2 3 4-2 1 0 9
Printed in Hong Kong by
EVERBEST PRINTING COMPANY LIMITED

Introduction
by Martin Keen

It would be foolish to attempt a Foreword to this book that would please everyone who knows the Bruce Trail at first-hand. If I were to describe the view from Rattlesnake Point as being the most spectacular on the Trail, some other well-seasoned hiker might counter with the virtues of the caves at Halfway Rock Point. Were I to devote too many words to the beauty of the rare orchids that are to be found along the sides of the Trail, I would probably irritate by default those whose greatest delight is to treasure the taste of the pure waters of Georgian Bay. It is not a lack of space or words that puts complete description beyond my reach. My problem is quite simply that the Bruce Trail means so many different things to so many different people.

    The Trail is not a route that was made by nature. Nor was it blazed out by Indians or early settlers. It has no long, romantic history. In fact it did not exist as such until 1967 and was the final culmination of many years' enthusiastic work on the part of a group of Ontario naturalists. Today the Trail winds for some 430 miles, from Queenston Heights near Niagara, to Tobermory at the tip of the Bruce Peninsula. It is comprised of eleven sections. Each one has been cleared and is maintained by a chapter of the Bruce Trail Association.

    The natural guideline for the Trail is provided by the Niagara Escarpment, a limestone promontory that runs erratically and jaggedly from central Michigan to Manitoulin Island. At some places the Trail cuts through dense brush and forest. Frequently it angles down the rugged face of the escarpment. It crosses over and under major highways and at several points follows the sidewalks of rural towns.

Recorded in the logs of the Bruce Trail Association are the names of about 175 hearty souls who have walked every foot of the way, from one end of the Trail to the other. James Staudacher, an 'end-to-ender' from Milwaukee, Wisconsin, wrote on his first day out of Tobermory: 'The mud was ankle deep and as slick as ice. My feet squished and squashed inside my boots . . . every few minutes we had to stop and empty the water from them.' But a month later, as he approached the cairn at Brock's Monument, he wrote: 'We walked through miles of fragrant vineyards and orchards. One afternoon we picked and ate wild strawberries and cherries. That same evening we explored some old forts and monuments of the War of 1812. All too soon we approached the end of the Trail.' Perhaps it is this very variety, with all its oddities, charms and complexities, that makes the Trail one of the most appealing to hikers in all North America. But of no less reward to those who founded the Trail is the enjoyment it gives to hundreds of families who may be found, with their cars parked at one point or another along the way, and who are just out for a Sunday of fresh air and a look at the beauties of nature.

Don't hope to leave this book thinking that you have a grasp of the Trail in all its length and wonder. Consider this book to be only a hint, only a glimpse of what awaits you through the thickets, over the fields, down the streets and up the cliffs of the Bruce Trail.

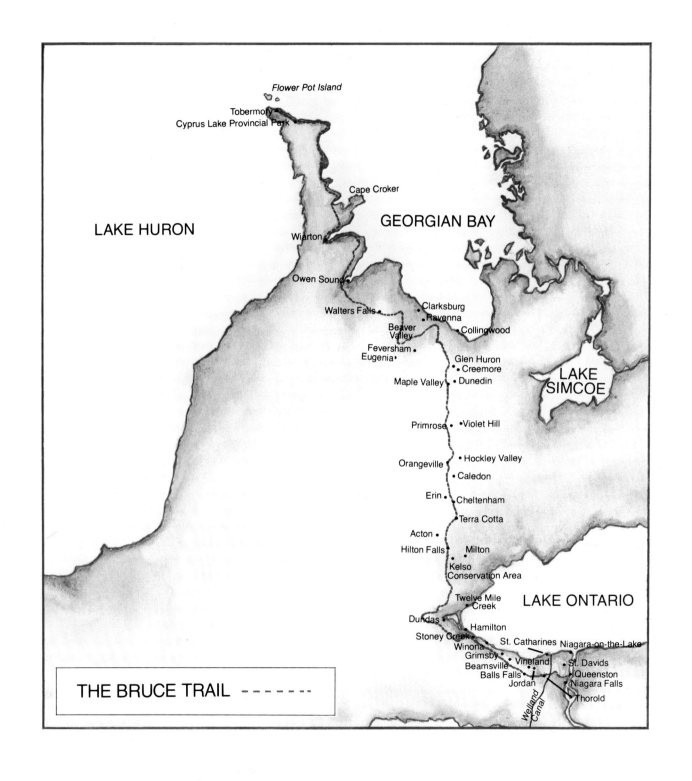

Flower Pot Island

Tobermory
Cyprus Lake Provincial Park

Cape Croker

LAKE HURON

GEORGIAN BAY

Wiarton

Owen Sound

Walters Falls
Clarksburg
Ravenna
Beaver
Valley
Collingwood

Feversham
Eugenia
Glen Huron
Creemore

Maple Valley
Dunedin

LAKE
SIMCOE

Primrose
Violet Hill

Orangeville
Hockley Valley

Caledon

Erin
Cheltenham

Terra Cotta

Acton
Hilton Falls
Milton

Kelso
Conservation Area

LAKE ONTARIO

Twelve Mile
Creek

Dundas
Hamilton

Stoney Creek
St. Catharines
Niagara-on-the-Lake

Winona
Grimsby
Vineland

Beamsville
St. Davids

Balls Falls
Queenston

Jordan
Niagara Falls

Welland
Canal
Thorold

THE BRUCE TRAIL – – – – – –

1 Dogwood violets

2 Trillium patch near Wiarton

3 Brock's Monument,
Queenston

6 Niagara-on-the-Lake
7 Niagara-on-the-Lake

8 Plum blossoms, St. Davids

9 Pigeon loft, Dundurn Castle,
Hamilton

10 Grape Harvest, Beamsville
11 Grape Harvest, Beamsville

12   Harvard Formation of
Canadian Warplane Heritage
near Jordan

13   Kelso Conservation Area

14   Dundurn Castle, Hamilton

15   Highway 8, Grimsby

16   Highway 8, Grimsby

17 Colonel Robert Nelles' home,
Grimsby

18 Highway 8, Grimsby

19 Balls Falls Conservation
Area, Jordan

20 Fishing on Twelve Mile
Creek south of Milton

21   Skylon tower, Niagara Falls

22   Niagara Falls, winter sunrise

23 Whirlpool Rapids Cable Car,
Niagara Falls

24 Niagara Gorge near
Queenston

25 Winter greenhouse, Stoney Creek

26 Frost patterns on greenhouse at Stoney Creek

(over)

27 Spring flooding, Beaver Valley near Eugenia

28 St. Davids, spring farm scene
29 Queenston

30 Grape vines in spring, Beamsville

31 Plum orchard in blossom, St. Davids

32 Henley course near St. Catharines
33 near Violet Hill

34   P-51 Mustangs gathered for
Hamilton Air Show

35   Racing through the streets
of Hamilton

36 Farm near Creemore

37 near Owen Sound

38 Church south of Walters Falls
39 Limestone cliff (Beaver Valley)
(over)
40 Clarksburg apple orchard

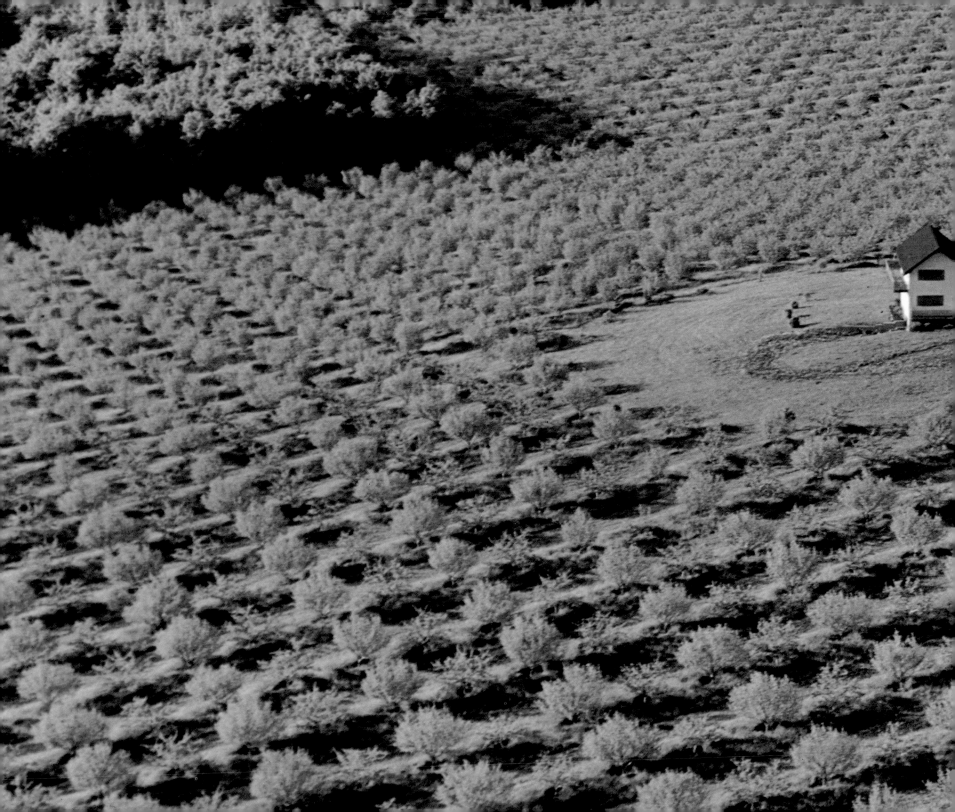

41 Twelve Mile Creek harbour
42 Niagara-on-the-Lake marina

43   Flower Pot Island lighthouse

44   Tobermory Harbour at dawn

45   Cedar trees clinging to
limestone rock at Hilton Falls
46   Flower Pot Island

47 The *Chi-Cheemaun* at Tobermory

48 Overhanging Point, Cyprus Lake Provincial Park

49 Halfway Point Rock,
Cyprus Lake Provincial Park

50 Divers at Halfway Point Rock,
Cyprus Lake Provincial Park

51 Racoon near Tobermory

52 near Collingwood

(over)

53 Sunset near Cape Croker

54 Farm yard at Caledon

55 Log building, Balls Falls

56 Farm near Dunedin
57 Twenty Mile Creek near Jordan

58 near Vineland

59 Autumn colour near Orangeville

60 Chicken judging,
Feversham Fall Fair

61 Erin Fall Fair

62 near Terra Cotta

63 Caledon Hunt Club

64 near Cheltenham

65 near Beamsville

66 Pumpkins near Winona

67 Highway 8, market near
Stoney Creek

68 near Glen Huron

69 Freak snow fall,
Thanksgiving Day, Collingwood

70 Fruit baskets, Grimsby

71 Abandoned farmhouse near Ravenna

72 Halton Region Conservation area at Milton

73 Cedar rail fence in the Hockley Valley

74 Collingwood Winter Carnival at Blue Mountain

75 Professional ski racing, Blue Mountain, Labatt's Pro Race

76 Collingwood Shipyard

77 Collingwood Terminals Elevator

78 St. Catharines shoreline, Lake Ontario

79 near Primrose

80   near Maple Valley

81   Icicles and shadows near Grimsby

(over)

82   Derelict barn near Acton